THE
TELEPHONE BOOK

The Telephone Book

1877

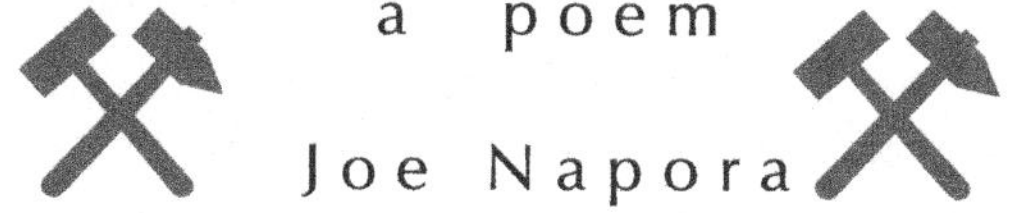

a poem

Joe Napora

Acknowledgements:

Selections published in A Magazine; Giants Play Well in the Drizzle; Pemmican, an annual of poetry; Shattered Wig Review; and a selection titled "The International Operator" in the anthology Generations A Centenary of American Poets (1919-2019), also in A World Without Wars: Overthrowing Capitalism Volume Six.

2021 © Joe Napora
ISBN: 9781736419823

BullHead Books 509 North Main #1 Piqua Ohio 45356

The Illustrations

The clip art of hammers and nails comes from the Swift Publisher software used to produce this book. The engravings are used with permission from *Pictorial Webster's Pocket Dictionary* by John M. Carrera. These reproductions from the 1898 original *Webster's International Dictionary* are more than copies. Carrera explains: "That fall [after an exhibit at the Smithsonian] I embarked on a ten-year odyssey that culminated in a book called *Pictorial Webster's* printed by hand on a letterpress from the original engravings and bound by hand...." His resulting book, though, is more than a work of art and craft. The book is patterned and, as he writes, "may be used to unlock your own innermost thoughts or help spark your imagination... Because, truly, everything in the universe is connected somehow; it's just a question of figuring out the connection." The cover photo of the author and grandson Wilder Napora is by grandson Gable Napora.

Dedicated to Barbara for answering that first call

> W oe
> to the man
> who invokes
> the antagonism
> of priests
> and property
>
> –Walt Whitman
>
> From an 1877 Address:
> "In Memory of Thomas Paine"
> at Lincoln Hall in Philadelphia

Hello. Help you? Yes. That is correct. Meridel Le Sueur's mother Marian Wharton was born in 1877.

Phoney — "as unreal as a telephone conversation" (1910 dictionary)

My first memory of the telephone, before then it must have only been another household fixture, just as our coal stove was only furniture until I burned my fingers on it, my first memory of it was when I received a call, and my mother handed me the phone saying it was a friend of mine. Instead of answering immediately I listened, and the longer I waited to speak the more foolish I felt at not talking, thinking that I could begin at any time to start up the conversation, could say "Hello" and he would never know I had been holding the phone for minutes just listening. And listening to what? The silence and the hint of a possible breathing which could have been my friend on the other end of the line, and if it was the telephone itself that was alive I was not convinced thereby that suddenly machines were becoming humanized. The opposite. That breathing. I recalled it from dreaming, a story told after the lights had gone out, a bad tv show, a nightmare.

I think I realized then that these machines are not extensions of ourselves except at the loss of ourselves. I hung up the phone, told my mother no one was there.

No one. None. O. The loss. I can see it, see through it.
I said, "I'll go over to his house and talk to him."

The year 1877 is . . . .

1877

... Brute beauty and valour and act, oh, air, pride, plume, here
Buckle! AND the fire that breaks from thee then, a billion
Times told lovelier, more dangerous, O my chevalier!

—Gerald Manley Hopkins, "The Windhover" (May 30, 1877)

The year 1877 is a case in point. It was the heyday of
conservative philosophy (let people fend for themselves), and
that summer in the hot cities, where poor families lived in
cellars and drank infested water, their children got sick.
— Howard Zinn, *The Politics of History*.

18771877187718771877187718771877187

1877:January

In on the

crumbled paper smuggled out
on the paper crumbled, torn
from the toilet roll
of the prison cell, split, ripped
said the former defense minister

the thugs have seized the means
of consumption
the message the message was broad
it was cast like styrofoam
on the waters

the waves of the waters
broadcast in the foam in the form
of a commercial —

It was a long long line and everything was in it all the facts first
and all the sounds the singing and shouting weeping and
laughing the pain was in there and all the hope we had and there
was an emptiness and we need it the emptiness there it must be
in there or the history is a lie it was unless the line of dead in

January—The Boston and Maine Railroad cuts wages by
10 % in '86 after a 6% dividend, the board raised the

We Control

the Spare Parts Stand By
For Your First Metal Breakdown

(...after the coup the CIA suggested that IT&T
change that irritating busy signal to a
computerized subliminal
musical message: We Are Never
Too Busy For You)

E-E-E-E-E-E-E-E-E-E-E-E-E-E-E-E-E-E-E-E-E-E-E-E
changed to AYE, ahh

Oh you kidder.
Bells. Balls. The difference is only a sound
effect. Small change. To send him to The School
of the Americas. Graduation Day.
The uniform.
The torturer smiles.
CLANG & BANG.
SLICE & DICE.

cemeteries to save the union we were told so we kept it all in so it
was a long line and everything was in it and it was Captain
Wurtz Captain Wurtz shouting Now boys slash em like lightning
the clubs descended and ascended otherwise it is prose all the
superfluous words must go to be pared away to reveal reveal the

salaries of its president and superintendent. January 4—
Cornelius Vanderbilt died. His estate worth more than all the

Change

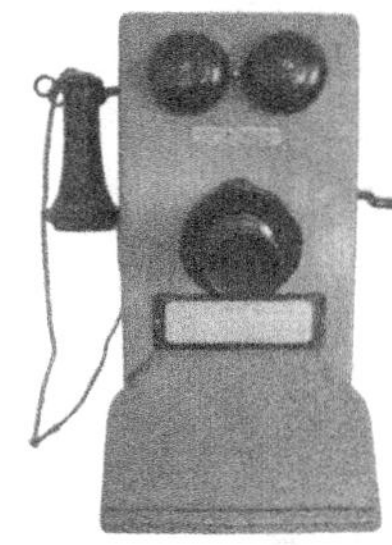

the economy
in his mind. Quite literally
so very shocking. But
you are not. You are not, the Chairman
he said, Martin S. David,
of Gulf & Western: You can't be
emotionally bound to any
particular asset. And Nixon say –
be lovingly. We will squeeze
Chile's economy until it screams
Electrodes rushed South in
diplomatic pouches. K.
He smile.   Kiss.
TV.   In (te)
Broken. Ger.
Finger. (Up
yours you corporate lackey!)
Up. Up yours.

You. *you   y o u*

- -

deep image the cutting image to clearly presented in its outline
that it cuts and hurts the mind the police become to look too
much like the school teachers rulers smacked across knuckles
every stroke hit a new head whose owner went solid to the
ground or bowled in continual somersaults concussions brain

- -

money in the US Treasury. January 15 — Lewis M.
Terman, psychologist developed Stanford-Binet IQ test.

"Wait! Wait."

Not in this poem.
Not a thousand points of light.
Not sparklers applied to skin.
Not words that burn misshapened.
Not worries feeding fear. Miss happened.
Not warts. Farts.
Not worms. Forms shaping miseries.
Not Where, where are we?
Not words sharpened.
Not words shaped to make a point.

The long distance operator is every writer
so that any of us, every reader
is connected through the emptiness
of the other.

It is writing that joins us
as it cuts us.
Not a line
of the type
to carry us further

rattled here's the word through I'm all shook up and we spell it
thru not thinking of what we've lost in our desire for speed for a
shorthand to use in poetry and advertising the officers seemed to
put their whole soul into this community work which is why the
image itself has no meaning we lose the sensual quality of the

February 12—The 1st news dispatch by telephone was
made, Boston to Salem, Mass. February 12—The

not intimate
to a life lived, and
face to sweaty face.

Sitting on a Wire

a black bird
's claws
wrapped in a
circle closes in

to a noise squeezing
cutting off into
a gasp the last
song of a man condemned
to never know that

as he falls down
into himself the pain

word the ough *ough* and because is is not necessary is reason to
keep the curves of the o g and h every thing is a relation the book
is a boat and the ship always contains you and the words you
carry carry or you watch yourself left alone on the no-man island
island death is not the great leveler not a substitution for the

Brotherhood of Locomotive Engineers stop trains in New
England. Boston police called in to break the strike.

he says is the poem
no one not there
is now listening
does he care?

O yes

He is that kind of fool
with a gun
and he's begun
to harvest bankers
and politicians.

In America

Is there an "R"?
Draw the head.
Is there an "rr"?
Draw the eyes.
Is there a "roar", a "road," a risk
in asking when will it end? This
refusal of revolution.

bogeyman or for paradise death is a hierarchy the poor
dying with a dream of some future reward and the rich die
in comfort with supreme pleasure Nelson Rockefeller died in
the arms of his mistress while laying on top of her pumping
his oil into her then he dried up but he was fine dying died

February 20—The 1st cantilever bridge in US was
completed at Harrodsburg, Kentucky. March 2, Republican

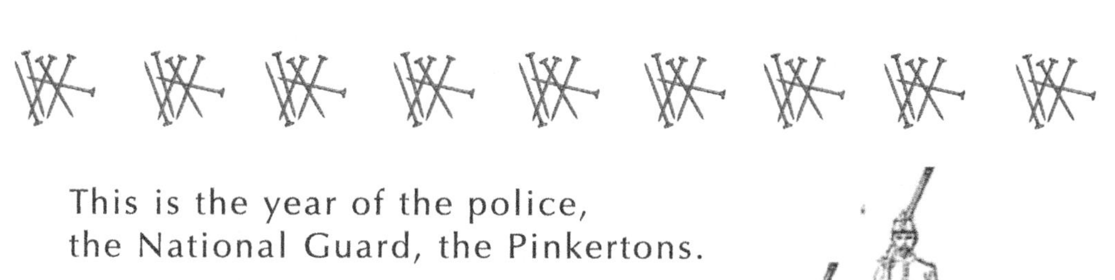

This is the year of the police,
the National Guard, the Pinkertons.

Draw the clouds, the gas, and
draw tears in the eyes.
Draw yours.
Are the eyes dots? Lines? Lies?
Do the eyes see?
The eyes bulge out and the mouth
is not yet a slit
across the face.

very happy what better way to go my high school buddy died
sitting in a helicopter in Vietnam writhing screaming
looking out as his enemies approached with guns and grins
there is no hereafter only now that hurts and the death of
nature is advertised as a tv special with millions connected

Rutherford B. Hayes was declared winner of the 1876
presidential election over Democrat Samuel J. Tilden, even

around the world Live Aid from Baltimore to Bangladesh
pressing buttons on their telephone visa card to save the
farms the rain forest the children to save the idea of the
natural but says the phone operator displace from her job by
a talkative and reliable computer all you need is love and she

though Tilden had won the popular vote 50.1 to 47.95%.
March 9—President John Garrent of the B&O Railroad,

The cock rises useless
and the sky shivers.
The rope tightens.

This is the year of the perfect silence.
This is the year the railroad veins
 broke upon the land. Bleeds. There.
Draw your own arms, legs. There

there is a poem that remains to be
written. There are no fingers
on the hanging man.
This man who is only a Hand.
Who understands the game
to be played by the bossman.

There is a poem that begins
and contains with it the names
of all the betrayers. Yet.
There is a poem
within. The pieces

deposits 25 cents to cover the copyright of the words to the
estate of John Lennon meanwhile the lines in places grow
shorter people are dropping off like the RAID lab testing
site, spray guns liquidating the varmints mostly women
and children winding their way through the mountains

William H. Vanderbilt, son of Cornelius, Hugh J. Jewett
of the Erie Railroad, Thomas A. Scott of the

the pieces are sharp fragments of a mirror
reflecting madness and your dying.
The remains. Discards
and desolation of the names
trash upon the landscape
dazzling the eye with the spectacle
of consumption and fear. Take
and make the R.

The "R" was a roar and a road and a risk.
And the mouth is open and crying.
I can write only the beginning
of half a poem of a man hanging
and it's weights they use from knots
tied to his testicles. Harold Green

president of IT&T, Henry Kissinger,
Secretary of State William Rodgers, and
John McCone former head of the CIA
and vice president of IT&T talk

trying to find some refuge with Sitting Bull's people in
Canada it was freedom of choice all along the way they could
choose to die or they could choose to live the rest of their
natural lives in prison for some of them sitting there in that
soccer stadium in Santiago it was not as easy as you might

Pennsylvania Railroad conspire to break the unions.
March 10—First Anniversary of Alexander Bell's famous

they talk back and forth and for
the back alley conspiracy
to prevent the inauguration
of Salvatore Allende,
The weight swings and the man screams
but the secret conversation drowns
out the words of one man dying. Theirs
is half a conversation

that continues long distance the line
they fill with money
to a soccer field in Santiago. They
talk and the wires
all along the line of shadows
of lines of words
slivers hardened into glass fall
falling down from the telephone
wires. Down to the playing field.
Tinkle. Tinkle.
Believe me.
It's not Christmas.

think they were mightily confused the military had acted
so suddenly for once Washington had coordinated things
perfectly for others it was damn difficult since Canada
seemed the promised land even if it wasn't their land some
Indians at least had found some peace General Howard

"Mr. Watson, come here I want you." March 18—Edgar
Cayce, psychic, was born in Hopkinsville, Kentucky.

This is the Killing Field

This is where the nameless one are being
executed and where Victor Hara
sings his songs that attempt to make the poem
whole. What
are the marks upon the paper?
The paper is *El Mercurio, La Prensa*.
The answer enables you
The answer enables you to put fingers on the
man condemned to die. There
are fingers and there are toes. A line
at a time. The line stretches him
and it stretches us all to the point
of some breaking. Somewhere midst
the fragments of pestilence
and of pain
the black and metal rain
drops from the name
Michael Vernon Townley
who will assassinate Letelier
in Washington with Kissinger's

told them we do not wish to interfere with your religion such
freedoms are guaranteed after all but you must talk about
practical things twenty times over you repeat that the earth
is your mother and about chieftainship from the earth let us
hear no more but come to business at once it was all about

April— First telephone wire connects the home of Charles
Williams Jr. of Somerville to his factory in Boston. April

God Bless You. 

In Spanish

There is this need for grieving.
In Spanish the guards they listen.
The guards beat out the message
In Spanish
the receiver is the board room 
it has a rhythm
a pounding of the blows
upon the singer. 
He the instrument.
Who? 

(Who did this? Who
did this to you!)

business let us hear no more Henry had no illusions about that
Nixon almost puked when Allende was elected democracy was
one thing but it was not the only thing Toohoolhoozote tried to
go on in his earlier vein you white people get together measure
the earth and then divide it part of the Indians gave up their

10—Federal troops were withdrawn from Columbia, South
Carolina. April 14—Brotherhood of Locomotive Engineers

In Spanish the man says, his last words—

We know who did this to our country.
We know who is the enemy.

"See-ya"

See-Ya.

    C-I-A. Echoes. seeya seeya seeya Echoes
through Yellowstone National Park
before bumper to bumper campers
and mini-vans, before Ansel Adams.
The calls went out for vigilantes
to track down Chief Joseph of the Pierced Noses
and his people the Army could not catch.

land I never did the earth well you can just imagine the
reaction these words got at the Security Council is part of my
body and I never gave up the earth General Howard sent a
telegram message to General McDowell in San Francisco think
we will make short work of it the Mollies were hanging of

orders a strike in Pennsylvania, crippling rail traffic
throughout the region. The newspapers had denounced

And
and he sang a song and a song of six pence,
a song, it was of sickness
and I imagine him, one solider, it only takes
a solitary man, he is stuck in his mess of a chase
while soldiers in the east shoot strikers
he must find the Indian
and he must kill him
but he levels his rifle
onto General Howard. And Kingsbury

said "That Wheatstone called the enchanted lyre
a telephone is a statement
which is to be found in most of the books
on the subject ...."

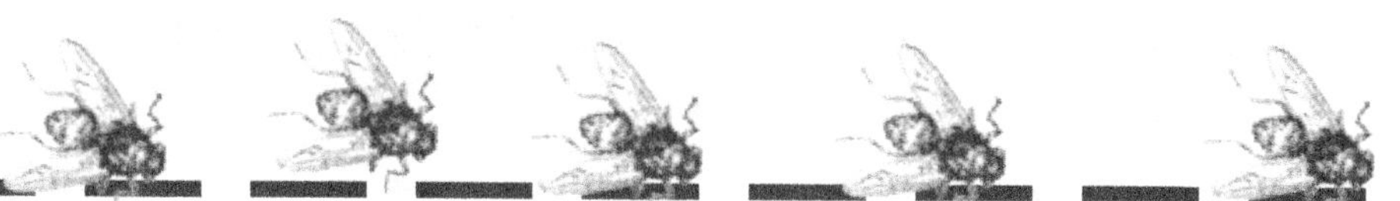

course short work the rebellion died down in the coal fields
and a movie was made about them with Richard Harris
playing the role of Jamie McFarland Pinkerton Detective
Agency operative and Sean Connery planting dynamite
 From 1964 to 1973, as part of the Secret War operation

the strike almost from the start and now only grew
more strident. "It is not surprising," the Iron Molders'

The Cord is Coiled

coiled about the neck
about the neck
and the nearly naked back
down the back

of the teenager reading
reading while she speaks
the love poems
poems of Pablo Neruda. Her lover
her lover hovers over a question
mark the smoke makes from his pipe
and he listens
listens at a pay phone in Bangkok.
He tries he attempts
he controls he conquers
to keep his body
his body from turning
turning into dust. His words
shuttering and shattering
against her body. The teenager

conducted during the Vietnam War, the US military dropped
260 million cluster bombs - about 2.5 million tons of
munitions - on Laos over the course of 580,000 bombing
missions I know you are going to think I made this up but I
swear that McFarland was the great great grandfather of Bill

Journal had remarked some months earlier, "that the press
of the country is against Trade Unions. It could hardly be

she gyrates
she gyrates her young
young and nervous hips
and hangs herself
hangs upside down
down over the living room couch.

It's party time.
It's the party line.
It's the universal
con-connection
in the city of mystics and opium
life and lies
ideologies disguised as mysteries
confuse ex-hippies and gurus. She
says
Jujus are candies
not enlightenment.

Casey can't you just see him telling the story of Ollie
North we were at the dance with Wacky acting foolish as
he always did this was long before he volunteered to go to
Vietnam always wanted to fly always wanted to die so the
rhyme goes anyway wanting to kill some gooks and it was

expected that the newspapers of an enemy, in any conflict,
would do justice to both sides. —Robert Bruce. April 30—

The general supported by Milton Friedman
and all those supply side
winder siders, a grinning and a hissin
O Yes Sire. The professors at Chicago.
O Yes. There is nothing wrong
with greed. It is our need.

She refused to hang up
the phone. She makes her own
connection. And

and the phonies
fall down afraid
of her beauty and her power. This

is not Dial-for-Dollars. This
is not Dial-a-Porn. It was

1-900-UFUCKME
that disconnected Victor Hara.

leaving Laos, a country approximately the size of Utah, with
the unfortunate distinction of being the most heavily bombed
country in history my generation was the one that had
learned to dive under our desks and wrap our arms over our
heads to protect ourselves from flying glass fragments when

Alice B. Toklas was born. May 6—Chief Crazy Horse
surrendered to U.S. troops in Nebraska. May 26—Isadora

The Messages Remain

hidden, gone underground to grow
into a living being. The being
is human. A miner. A worker who
knows
because his body knows
more than you know.

Living long after the man's frail form
is swept by the winds
swept by the winds that
carry with them
the lengthening reach
of their wings

the black birds of twilight
question. Asking
Asking?
How does the body react to pain?
Who is the Beast?
What exactly are its crimes?

the armory I thought it a strange place to have a dance but
I figured they had to use the building for something but I
never figured never even thought about why the building
was there in the first place why should I It is more than all
the bombs dropped on Europe throughout World War II,

Duncan, free form, interpretative dancer, was born in San
Francisco. June 1—U.S. troops pursue bandits into

It was Dial-a-Porn
that connected Nixon to the businessman
using the neon yellow banana phone.

That was his part.

For my part I do not see why a juggler with a speaking machine is a more culpable imposter than he who pretends to breath oil, or to make puppets speak, as in the Chinese shadows. — *History of Inventions*

Juggler: US Congress, Generals, TV Preachers, NPR, NBC, Ronald Reagan, Donald Trump, Bill Clinton, Margaret Thatcher
Breathe Oil: Exxon Valdez, Gulf, Arbusto Energy, Shell, Patriot Fuel
Puppets: Augusto Pinochet, Oliver North, Jose Duarte, Jerry Falwell, Dan Quayle,
Chinese Shadows: Tienaman Square, George Bush, Allen Dulles

the bomb went off I was looking up Mary Stewart's dress the dress it had slipped up over her pretty little bum and she had these little pink flowers on her underwear the music played and we were restless as only teenagers can be I doubt it but perhaps our bodies knew we were in the midst of the war

Mexico. June 17—Federal troops, loot and destroy a peaceful Nez Perce village that thought itself under

Anaconda

It is indeed the Reign of the Police.
And gradually the Anaconda of the Law
coils tighter and tighter.—Voltarine de Cleyre

A boa constrictor and a town and
a living plant made from copper and
sweat and the miseries of money
that talks, yells, screams, mumbles
oaths and curses and hope for
a life in the sky in the sky by and buy.
And yet the garbled sound is easier
to understand. It is the straight line
that is mystifying, terrifying. One word.
One thing. The exact thing
at the end of a string.
An easy and quick way
of dying. A line stretches by design
across two continents from the Mesabi Range
a copper wire weaves its way
through mountains

machine all over the Midwest the strikes were going on
the government response was simple armories were built
in nearly every city to protect the property from the
people then the Indian wars continued the governments
response was simple brick stockades were built in

Federal protection. June 21—Ten Molly McGuire
miners executed in Pennsylvania. Their crime was their

grass and jungles to the president's palace
in Santiago. This copper coil constricting
the blood of the miners of Minnesota and Utah
swallows the dreams of those who die young
in the pits of earth cut into the hills of Chile.

Let's say a phone rings running
underground right to your hand. This is no
pay phone. This is the Captain speaking.
Who would have the nerve
to hang up?

There are Bills to Pay.

Credit cards.
Crowds calling. Don't hang, don't hang.
Don't hang up on me.
And crows cawing, only because they must.

The Irish and the Swedes who scrub the pores

numerous places and then out to round up every Indian out
on a reservation the general wasted no time he dispatched a
message up ahead with orders for the howitzers and Gatling
guns to wheel toward the rim and open fire on the village I
found this letter and I guess it didn't surprise me much since

love for their brothers in the railroad union. July 2—
Federal troops defeated by Nez Perce warriors. July 2—

of their skin excavating minute
particles in a daily ritual of cleansing
visit the bars and whore houses of St. Paul
only dimly realizing that
the long distance operator
has connected them to their brothers
far to the south.

They speak but who hears?

The language is only known
through the opening of the body
and the shared pain and blood that feeds
the snake. The mouth that devours

is the serpent who enters the listener's ear
and burrows in the brain.

The mouth is never satisfied.
One tongue hisses another caresses,
but the mouth is mind and the heart

she had to have been mightily impressed with the idea and
its partial realization of communication across great
distance making this intimate connection of the human
voice without the necessity of the physical presence of the
person being there and of course for her the person was

Herman Hesse born. July 11— Battle of Clearwater,
another military defeat of U. S. Army troops by the Nez

is the mouth that lisps
words someday to the depths
of desire. For at this depth
we do not vote in the slavers.
For at this depth we do not
condemn our children's future.
At this depth we do not
confuse the language of love
with the language of the killers.

"...it is said that the transmission of sound in
wood was ingeniously demonstrated by
Wheatstone. His telephone consisted of long rods
of light pine," etc.—Kingsbury

These Dial Phones are Obsolete

and so we torture ourselves
with static and love.
Once upon a time

always there and the letter is from Helen Keller to Alexander
Graham Bell dear Mr Bell I love you but the Indians their
losses at the Big Hole had also been high between sixty and
ninety Nez Perces had lost their lives including twelve of the
best warriors most of the casualties had been women and

Perce. July 17—U. S. troops sent to Martinsburg, West
Virginia to put down the railroad strike, nine strikers

I begin up

and on a time worn
weathered rack.
Fingers stuck
into holes.

Inside.
Did you doubt?

I'm coming.
A wheel spinning back
to its beginning
point. An arrow
through the heart. Or
maybe the beautiful lady
in red tights and
the knife flying toward her
spinning out of control. For

there is no escape

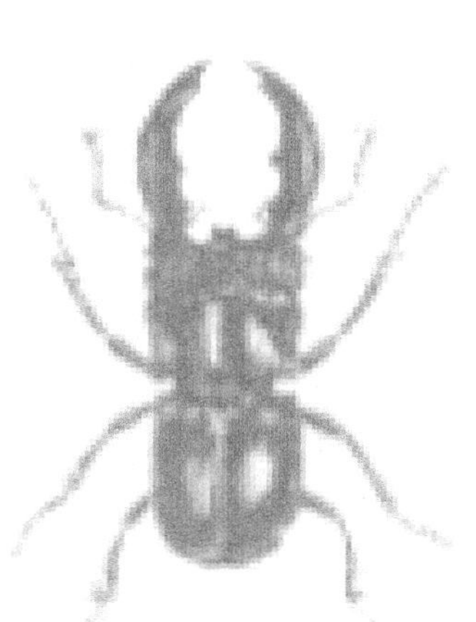

children slain during the attack on the tipis it didn't
surprise me very little of what the government does
surprises me anymore and now no longer being surprised
doesn't surprise me and I think that is the dilemma for me
as a parent I don't want the kids to grow up cynical and

killed. July 18—President Rutherford B. Hayes sends
the Second U. S. Artillery to Martinsburg to break the

through the words
or the words
if Cupid turns out to be
a policeman
with a long memory.

It is Grave

yards, it is the mine
my fathers labored in
and gave to me. A life
underground. They
kept their heads down
a hand on a shovel.
A hand in a fist. Stooped
in tunnels that snaked
under the river Monongahela.
And where two rivers meet
there

uncaring without ideals I want them to believe that this is
indeed the land of the free and the home of the brave and
when they find out what the government is really about I
want them to protest to close the gap between the language
and the reality and so when the politicians mouth all those

strike. July 18—Thomas Edison recorded the human voice
for the first time. July 21—In West Virginia 26 railroad strikers

the Indian mounds.
They buried the people
with their wings on.
They set them loose
to the land of the West.
The put themselves
to rest.

All the birds are not passenger pigeons
there are angles and angels
nor it is necessary to kill
the messenger. Anger. Life

goes on. And on. And yes.

It's a bad connection.
Where is static when we need it?
Here is the noise.
The Ornamental Receiver
and the Ornamental Transmitter,
this phone is not necessarily
phony. Remember

pieties to justify their war on the poor I try to see the
positive side of it that those words will someday come back
fully realized the truth will hurt that the poor will inherit
the earth that is as the chief said it is my body my body
and the strikers knew it too they closed this country this

were killed. July 25—Hayes orders six companies of
troops to Chicago. Six companies. Six. Six.

the slick stream
lined path of the bullet.
The steady hand. The trained
touch upon the trigger.

The nests, sometimes
five or six in a single tree,
Sycamore, and I slipped out
of the canoe and midst the feathers
and shit found the leg bones
of the herons. Hollow bones

they give themselves
to the hands that can
fashion them into forms
for music. Instead

I made pens,
for friends. For us. For each
to reach. To us.

---

country down and made the power mongers shiver and shake
in fear and face the truth that they had even hidden from
themselves that the government exists for the army and the
army exists for to protect the wealthy a moment of truth
should never be ignored and the Nez Perces had always been

July 26 —Reading, Pennsylvania occupied by federal
troops. July 28—Strike in East St. Louis broken by

The Image

in the poem deep into the
scars scares.
The concentrated power.

The greed. Lust.
Distance. Longing.
The burns
the wire makes
on the nipples. God

it is not fair
to play with words
but a fowl
the poetics of the vulture
and the shrike impales the
songbird
on the thorn. It is us

we—our soldiers

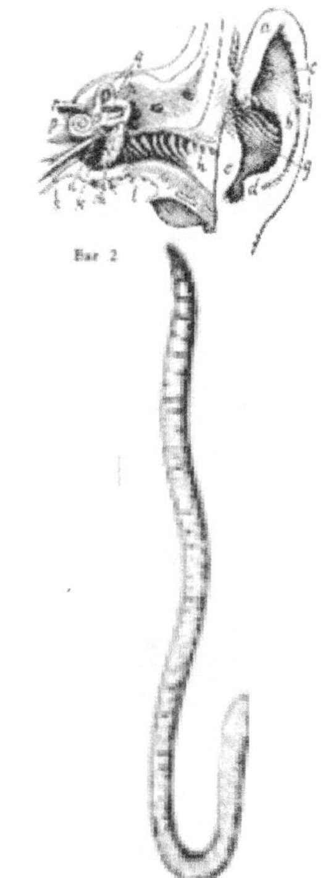

friendly to Montana whites and some of them had become
acquaintances of various farmers and merchants on
occasion while men had invited Nez Perces into their
homes to share meals with their families and all of this
midst the pursuit by the military to save face the army

federal troops. In America, at Boston and Cleveland,
Ohio dwelling houses and places of business are

who are out teachers—
are them with technology.
The rebels cannot escape
since the police are organized
across boundaries. We give them

the radios and computers. The
Israeli secret police connect
Guatemala City
to Jerusalem. We plan to make
these people obsolete. The
phone

rings reign.
In our desire for justice
we get the busy signal
a chirping of the computer
it is a locust of a memory
fading after a time

just had to capture them the bombs well they had to fall onto
the village and I don't blame my buddies who went to war
pulled the villagers out of the hootches from their own fear
and shot them then the flame throwers I think the main
reason I avoided the draft was so that I didn't have to cut my

connected with the telephone with a central office.
Merchants talk with each other with out the intervention

a time after all
when we learn to talk
and connect ourselves
to our bodies.

No Invention Goes Unused

which is why the god suggested Adam
sharpen the nails of his fingers
a weapon to cut flesh
to cut words into stone.
The memory fails.
The bombs fall.
The hot line.
No poems
about poems sizzle into splendor
with an urgency unmistakable
even in the darkness
of these days. The smoke rises

in a continual message of distant pain.

hair I have these big ears and I would have looked pretty
damn silly with my head buzzed it was that simple I
played war games all the time played with little plastic
men with their little plastic guns but mostly I played
cowboys and Indians and I never thought of it then but

of a third party, and therefore in perfect secrecy. –
Glasgow Herald. August 10, Col. John Gibbon

Scorched flesh leaves scars that suggest
stories enjoyed by congressmen
and bankers, hunters sharing secrets
at the lodge. The line
is that the president wants his old enemy
to share the peace prize. The line

is easy money for inside traders. Is
connecting Washington and Moscow
is a barbed wire fence
the corporate presidents do their dance upon
stretched through Latin America. And we

we who once only watched
watched in the paralysis of wonder
we slowly learn to talk
we imitate the sounds of the cries

the noises are the foundation
from this alphabet
made as the wire rips

neither the cowboys nor the Indians had crewcuts I
remember once I did persuade the barber to cut off all of my
hair my mother was furious she loved my curls it was the
last time a momentary lapse on my part but I was only a kid
maybe influenced by my uncle who sent back presents from

slaughtered Nez-Perce Indians at Big Hole River. September
5—Crazy Horse was fatally bayoneted by a soldier at Fort

pieces from our hands.

We help each other
tear it down.
In pieces, old broken
sentences, forever.

There is no one but
ourselves
to count on. The Russians
sold out the Sandinistas
for bunches of colored
beads, baubles, babbles,
burgers.

Even in a Fever My Son

who is barely one reaches

saying tutsch tutsch

the Korean war I got a silken jacket with a dragon
embroidered on the back he got appendicitis a few years later
and died in the hospital in Brownsville the general got the
New Perces the generals settled the strike and the trains
came through Allende died with the women and the men fight

Robinson, Nebraska. September 13—The Battle of
Canyon Creek. The Nez Perce escape; federal

his arm lifting and I
hold him up for his hand
to play along the light

switch or the chain
of the storm door. The heat
will pass. For now he warms me
In the night in the distance
it is light enough
to see the mercenaries.
The cold reality of things
gathers spirit with his sound
and the words he learns
are not names of objects
but activities made real
by resistance to this fingers
tutsch tutsch

And the many meanings of the
words
all words do not
disturb him or me.

with him Neruda was dead a few days later the assassins
were stalking Washington and set the bomb to Ronnie
Moffit's car the president was conspiring with Kissinger and
Colby about how to get re-elected and I was living then on a
farm in New Brunswick, Canada.

government ridiculed by Eastern newspapers. October 4—
Pancho Villa was born. October 15—Chief Joseph of the

This is a time for singing
and a time for grieving.
It's this party line. This
free for all. Better this
than all this bleeding.

We talk the way we know
how to talk.

And then we start
and we will
will be All.

Nez Perce surrenders. Chief White Bird leads the
remainder of the tribe to safety in Canada. December 6

—Thomas A. Edison made the first sound-recording when he recited "Mary had a Little Lamb" into his phonograph

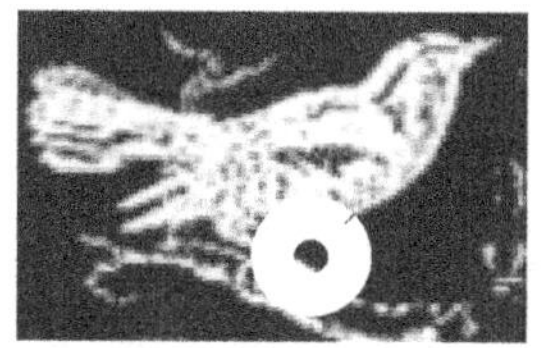

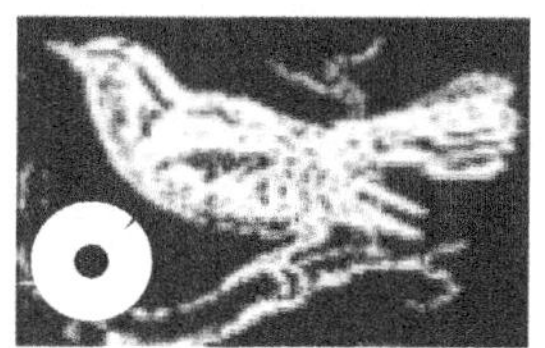

machine. Cezanne painted "Mme. Cezanne in a
Red Armchair." December 31, shortly after six
o'clock Gustave Courbet dies.

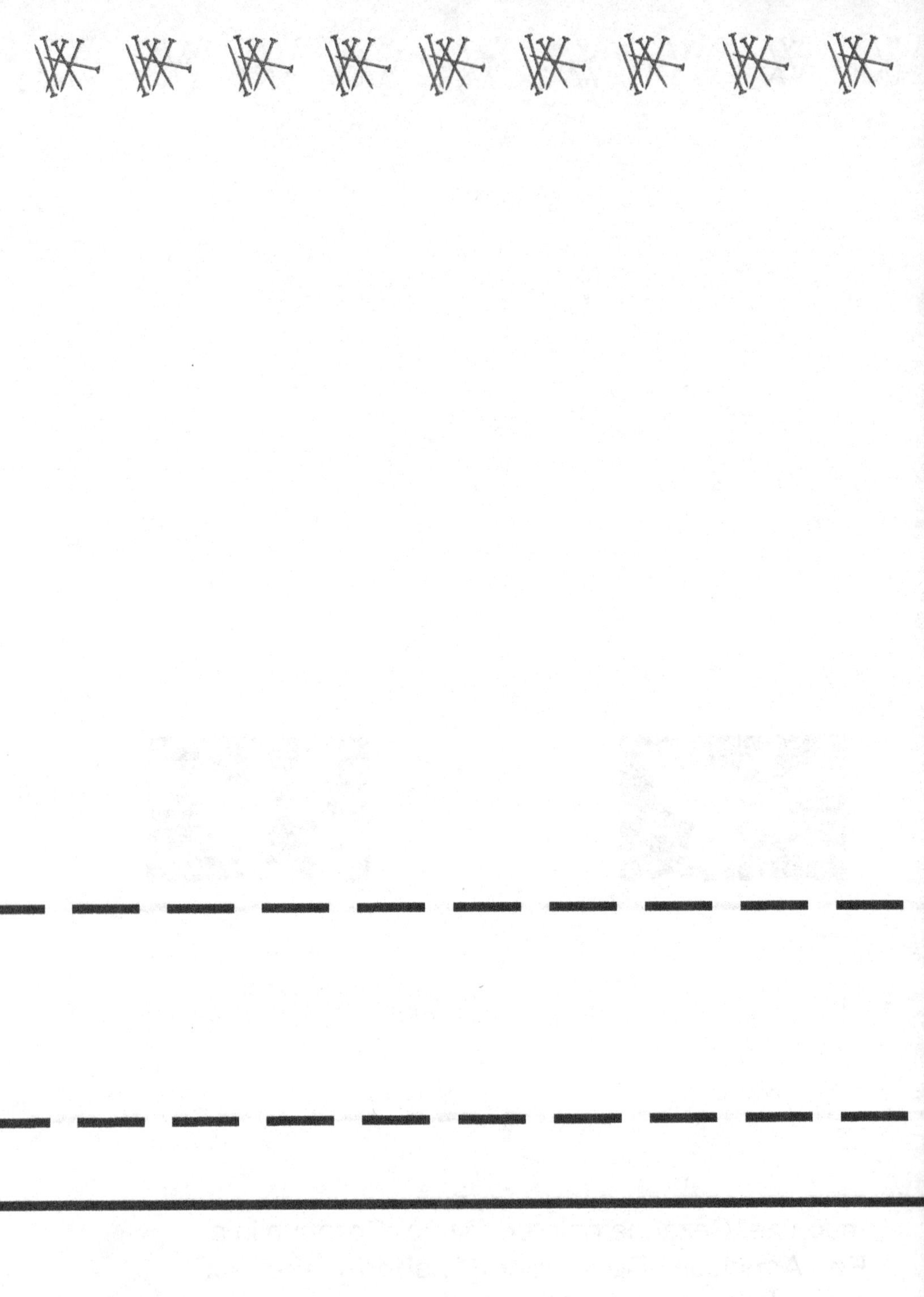

[46]

NOTE:

This poem was begun in 1981, revised in 2005, revised again in 2017. And again in 2021. Some of the references to the telephone are archaic now: the wires that once were ubiquitous, the circular dial phone, party lines, the monopoly by IT & T (International Telephone and Telegraph Corporation). What was the only US telephone company now has competition, but once it had none, certainly none for its role in the 1964 military coup against Joao Goulart the president of Brazil and the support for the Pinochet coup in Chile in 1973. These corporate crimes have faded in the collective memory. Even less known is the fraud of the election of Rutherford B. Hayes as President in1876, losing the popular vote to Democrat Samuel Tilden. Until the selection of George Bush by the Supreme Court, and the election of Donald Trump, the Hayes election was the nation's most controversial with, according to historians, Republican party members "under indictment for falsifying the Presidential election returns—and those returns had been essential for Hayes's electoral majority".

This is the end / Beautiful friend / This is the end /

My only friend

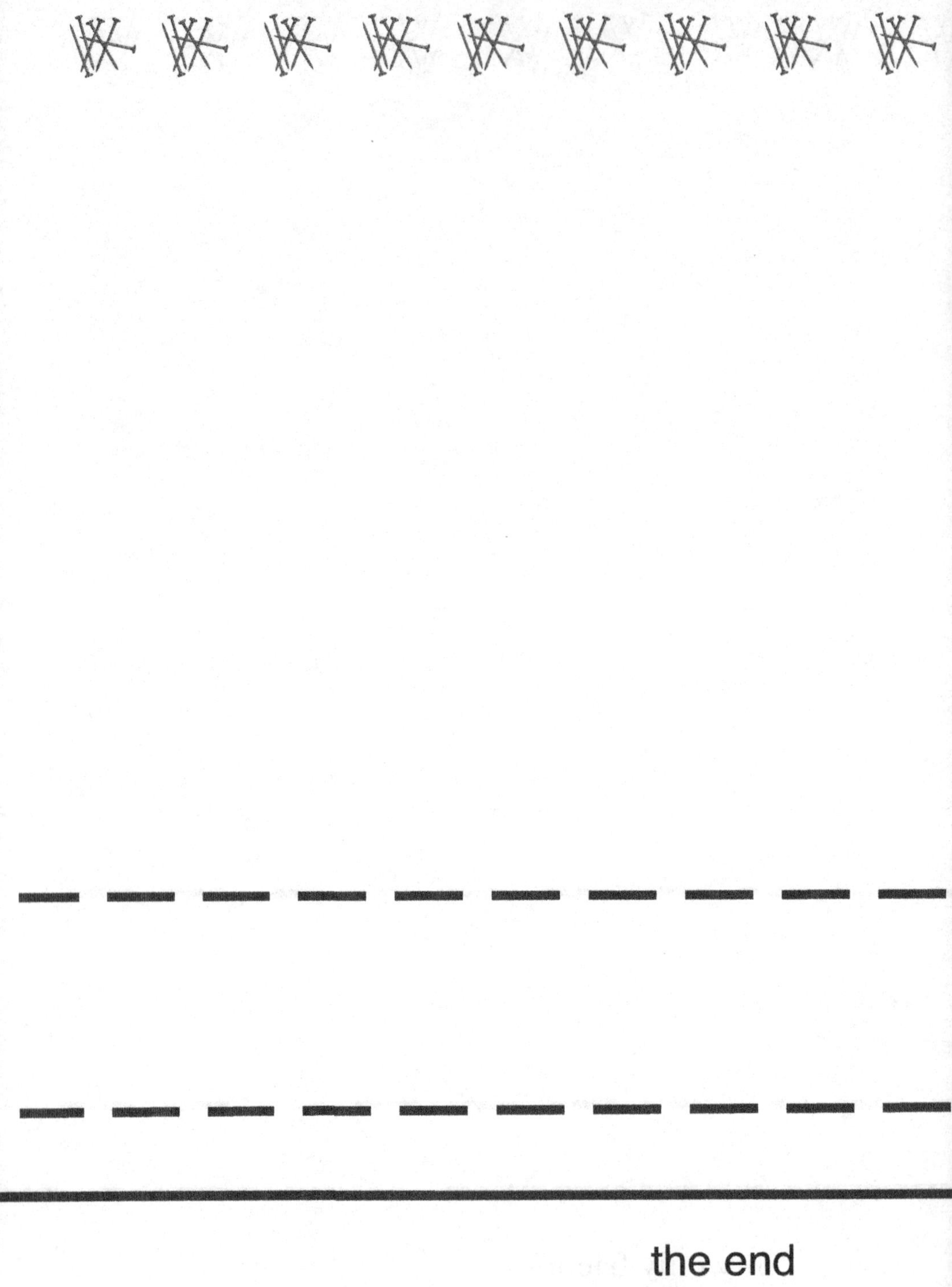

the end

Made in the USA
Monee, IL
07 July 2026

56550987R00031